UNSOLVED QUESTIONS ABOUT THE HUMAN BODY

BY MYRA FAYE TURNER

CAPSTONE PRESS
a capstone imprint

Published by Capstone Press, an imprint of Capstone
1710 Roe Crest Drive
North Mankato, Minnesota 56003
capstonepub.com

Library of Congress Cataloging-in-Publication Data
Names: Turner, Myra Faye, author.
Title: Unsolved questions about the human body / by Myra Faye Turner.
Description: North Mankato, Minnesota : Capstone Press, [2023] | Series: Unsolved science | Includes bibliographical references and index. | Audience: Ages 8–11 | Audience: Grades 4–6 | Summary: "Why do we yawn? Are left-handed people more creative? Why do we have fingerprints? When it comes to our bodies, there are a whole lot of questions we're still trying to answer. Get ready to explore the unknown and discover how scientists are working to solve the mysteries of the human body."—Provided by publisher.
Identifiers: LCCN 2022025138 (print) | LCCN 2022025139 (ebook) | ISBN 9781669002604 (hardcover) | ISBN 9781669002550 (paperback) | ISBN 9781669002567 (pdf) | ISBN 9781669002581 (kindle edition)
Subjects: LCSH: Human body—Juvenile literature. | Human physiology—Juvenile literature.
Classification: LCC QP37 .T84 2023 (print) | LCC QP37 (ebook) | DDC 612—dc23/eng/20220713
LC record available at https://lccn.loc.gov/2022025138
LC ebook record available at https://lccn.loc.gov/2022025139

Editorial Credits
Editor: Christopher Harbo; Designer: Sarah Bennett; Media Researcher: Svetlana Zhurkin; Production Specialist: Katy LaVigne

Image Credits
Getty Images: Ariel Skelley, 29, Camille Tokerud, 6, Daniel Grill, 18, Keystone, 23, Nick David, 28, yacobchuk, 22; Shutterstock: A3pfamily, 7, atanasis (background), cover and throughout, Bangkok Click Studio, 24, Dr Project (background), cover and throughout, Dragon Images, 11, Ezume Images, cover (bottom right), Friends Stock, 25, Gorodenkoff, 4, Halfpoint, 9, Maples Images, 16, MintImages, 13, Monkey Business Images, cover (top), 8, Nataly Studio, 27 (bottom), New Africa, 21, Oleksandr Bushko, cover (bottom middle), Pixel-Shot, 12, 14, Roongroj Sookjai, cover (bottom left), Stuart Monk, 17, szefei, 15, T.Photo, 26, wavebreakmedia, 19, Wirestock Creators, 27 (top)

Printed and bound in China 5132

TABLE OF CONTENTS

INTRODUCTION
The Amazing Human Body. 4

CHAPTER 1
Why Do We Laugh? 6

CHAPTER 2
Why Do We Dream? 10

CHAPTER 3
Why Do We Yawn? 14

CHAPTER 4
Are Left-Handed People More Creative? 18

CHAPTER 5
Why Do We Have Different Blood Types? 22

CHAPTER 6
Why Do We Have Fingerprints? 26

Glossary. 30
Read More 31
Internet Sites 31
Index 32
About the Author 32

Words in **bold** are in the glossary.

THE AMAZING HUMAN BODY

The human body contains many systems that work together. These systems make sure our bodies work the way they should. It's our job to take care of our bodies. But we do have some help. Doctors work to make sure we're healthy. Scientists research ways to fight and cure diseases.

| Scientists are always looking for the answers to the most puzzling questions about the human body.

Because of science, we know a lot about our bodies. For example, we know getting enough sleep is important to our health. Eating the right kinds of food helps our bodies and minds stay strong. But do we know why we dream? Why we laugh? Or even why we yawn? Get ready to explore these and other unsolved questions about the human body.

THE SCIENTIFIC METHOD

Scientists use a process called the scientific method to answer unsolved questions about the human body. They follow these steps:

- Ask a question
- Gather information
- Make a prediction
- Design an experiment to test the question
- Collect data
- Analyze data
- Draw conclusions
- Communicate results

CHAPTER 1

WHY DO WE LAUGH?

Everyone laughs. Humans start laughing as early as 3 months old. Babies born deaf laugh, even though they can't hear our funny jokes. Babies born blind can't see you make a silly face. But they giggle too.

Many people believe we only laugh because something pleases us. Studies show the opposite. We sometimes laugh at things that aren't funny at all. Researchers have investigated the science of laughter. They looked for the why behind our chuckles.

Not a lot of research has been done though. Why? Laughing makes us feel good. It's not harmful to our bodies. We aren't sure if it's helpful either. Scientists haven't narrowed down why we laugh. But they have a few ideas.

FACT Some animals, such as apes and rats, laugh too! But their laughter is different than the sound we make.

| Doing something fun, such as using a swing or going on amusement park rides, often makes us laugh.

| Laughing is contagious—in a good way! When someone you're near laughs, you're likely to laugh too.

Laughing isn't always about what tickles our funny bone. Instead, it's about our relationship with others. One study observed kids watching a cartoon. It discovered that kids laughed more when another child was in the room. Humans are likely to laugh when we see others around us laughing. If someone tells a joke and others laugh, we'll laugh too. Even if we don't get the joke.

Some people say, "laughter is the best medicine." Is this true? That's another **theory**. Laughing releases **endorphins**. These chemicals are released by the brain. They help us feel good. The feeling you get at the end of a race or when playing a sport is caused by endorphins too.

Some experts think laughing improves our health. Laughter increases oxygen intake, which gives us healthier hearts, lungs, and muscles. And a good laugh might boost our **immune systems**, which helps our bodies fight germs and diseases.

CHAPTER 2

WHY DO WE DREAM?

Do you remember your dreams? If not, that's okay. Most of us don't. When you sleep, parts of your body shut down. But not your brain. It keeps working.

Some dreams can be exciting, like ones about scoring the winning basket for your team. Other dreams are scary, like running from a fire-breathing dragon. Still, scientists are unsure why we dream or if it serves a purpose.

It may feel like we dream all night. But we only dream about two hours a night. Our bodies go through five stages of sleep. These stages are known as the sleep cycle. One of the stages is known as rapid eye movement, or REM, sleep. It is during this stage that we most often dream.

FACT You may enter REM sleep multiple times in one night. The first period usually happens about an hour and a half after you fall asleep. It lasts about 10 minutes.

| Sleep is an important part of living a healthy life. On average, children need about 10 to 12 hours of sleep each night.

One belief is dreams represent things we want. This is true even if we don't know we want them. You might dream your parents bought you a new bike, although a new bike wasn't on your mind.

SLEEPWALKING

Sleepwalking is when someone, who isn't fully awake, acts as if they are. The condition usually doesn't cause any harm. The person may look confused or not answer when spoken to. In some cases they could get hurt. For example, if they trip over something or fall down stairs. Adults have even driven cars while sleepwalking!

| Some people experience a sleep-related eating disorder (SRED) that causes them to eat while they sleep.

Some scientists think dreaming helps us make sense of information we've learned during the day. We may also dream as a way to review and then store away our memories.

Others say dreams are a way to practice solving problems. Let's say you are nervous about presenting a science fair project. Dreaming about giving an awesome presentation might help you prepare for it in real life.

| Giving the presentation of your dreams may actually start with dreaming about it the night before!

CHAPTER 3

WHY DO WE YAWN?

We yawn when we're bored. We yawn when we're tired or sleepy. Sometimes we yawn when someone else yawns. Even thinking about yawning could cause you to yawn. (Did you just yawn?)

| Yawning before going to bed may be a sign that your body is getting ready for sleep.

| Babies tend to yawn more times a day than older children and adults.

Some people think it's rude to yawn when someone else is talking. It suggests you're bored with the speaker. Of course, this isn't always true. Even unborn babies yawn. Yawning is an action we can't control. The question is *why* do we yawn? Scientists aren't sure.

One idea is yawning serves a social purpose. Babies yawn to let their parents know they're sleepy. Suppose you're watching a movie with your BFF. The movie is boring. So you start yawning. This could be a clue it's time for your pal to change the channel.

| On average, our yawns usually last about six seconds.

Yawning might be good for the body. One of the earliest beliefs is yawning helps our lungs. When we yawn we breathe in air. Then we let the air out. Some scientists concluded yawning removes any bad air we breathe in. This keeps our lungs healthy.

Yawning also causes an increase in blood pressure, heart rate, and the amount of **oxygen** in our blood. This improves **motor function**. So yawning might help wake us up when we're getting drowsy.

Finally, we might yawn to cool down our brains. Cool brains help us stay alert and function better. Our bodies have built-in ways to cool the brain if it overheats. It's possible yawning might help this process. Maybe yawning isn't so rude after all.

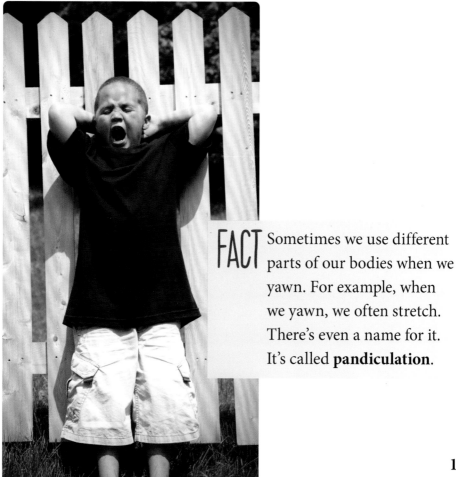

FACT Sometimes we use different parts of our bodies when we yawn. For example, when we yawn, we often stretch. There's even a name for it. It's called **pandiculation**.

CHAPTER 4

ARE LEFT-HANDED PEOPLE MORE CREATIVE?

Humans are born with a **dominant** hand. This is the hand we use for fine motor tasks, like writing. Most of us are right-handed. Only about 10 percent of people are left-handed. A small number—about one percent—are comfortable using either hand.

We don't choose if we're lefties or righties. We're just born that way. However, it's not until we're about 18 months old that we start favoring one hand over the other.

Some people have argued lefties are more creative than righties. Here's why. Our brains have two halves. Each side controls certain functions. For example, we use our left side for problem-solving, while the right side is the center of creativity.

| The left side of your brain may help with problem-solving, but both sides work together when you do math problems.

Here's where things get really interesting. The left—problem-solving—side of the brain controls the right side of the body. The right—creative—side of the brain controls the left side. Left-handed people should be more creative, right? That's what some people believe, but is it true? This question has been studied for years.

Lefties must learn early to live in a right-handed world. Most things are made with righties in mind. For example, can openers and cup handles are often made for the comfort of right-handed people. Lefties spend a lot of time solving problems. They have to figure out how to use objects not meant for them. This is why some researchers agree left-handed people are more creative. But there's no proof this is true.

FACT In 2019, researchers asked 20,000 people to rate how creative they were. Left-handed people rated themselves higher. However, there was no proof to support their claim.

One problem lefties face is how to use scissors that are designed for righties.

CHAPTER 5

WHY DO WE HAVE DIFFERENT BLOOD TYPES?

Everyone has red blood. But did you know people have different blood types? It's true. There are four major blood types: A, B, AB, and O. There are also many minor groups. There's "A positive," written as A+. Then there's "B negative," written as B-. AB+ is another group.

| Everyone's blood looks the same, but even siblings can have different blood types.

Doctors have known about blood types since the 1900s. Still, the reason *why* people have different blood types remains a mystery.

We know blood typing is important. Suppose you're in a serious accident. You need blood. Doctors might give you a **transfusion**. This is when one person's blood is pumped into another person's body. Before a transfusion, doctors need to know what type of blood to give you.

KARL LANDSTEINER

Karl Landsteiner was a doctor born in Vienna, Austria. In 1901, he was the first person to discover humans have different blood types. By 1909, he had grouped them into four major types. For his work, Landsteiner won the **Nobel Prize** in 1930.

Getting the wrong blood type would sound an alarm in your body. Your body would think it was under attack from something that could harm you. Your immune system would fight back. If you mix the same blood type from different people, it remains a liquid. If you mix blood from different groups, the blood clumps together. This could cause health problems. A person might bleed too much or have trouble breathing, for example.

FACT All humans can receive O- blood, no matter their blood type. For this reason, people with type O- are called **universal donors**. Their blood is in high demand at blood banks.

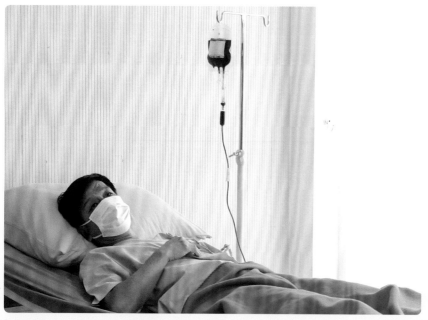

| Patients who need blood transfusions must be given a blood type that matches or is compatible with their own.

| Family members often share the same illness. But because of their different blood types, some of them may get better faster than others.

Which brings us back to our question. Why do we have different blood types? Some scientists believe different blood types formed over time as a way to fight disease. Different diseases attack certain blood types. If all our blood was the same, it's possible one disease could wipe out the whole human race.

WHY DO WE HAVE FINGERPRINTS?

In the movies, police sometimes use fingerprints to find the bad guys. This happens in the real world too. There's a reason police can identify prints left behind at the scene. But how is this possible? Believe it or not, each and every person has his or her own set of fingerprints. No two sets are the same. Even identical twins have different fingerprints.

| Fingerprints are a lot like snowflakes. No two in the whole world are exactly the same.

Fingerprints have different patterns. These shapes don't change as our fingers grow and get older. Even minor injuries won't alter your fingerprints. If you burn your fingers, for example, the skin will grow back. And your fingerprints will stay the same.

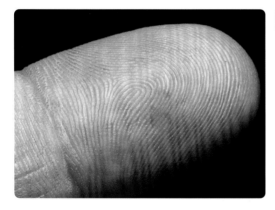

| A close-up view of a fingerprint reveals a complex pattern of raised ridges.

FINGERPRINT PATTERNS

Fingerprints come in eight patterns that include loops, arches, and swirly lines known as **whorls**. Each of our fingers have different print patterns. In fact, most fingers have more than one pattern. It's unusual for your fingerprints to have only one pattern.

| Fingerprints may help tell our brains that a cat's fur is soft when we pet it.

But why do we have fingerprints? Are they simply a way to identify one human from another? This is a mystery even the greatest detectives haven't solved.

Some people think we have these patterns at the tips of our fingers to help us grip objects better. Others believe they help with our sense of touch. They could help us identify when something is silky soft or rough like sandpaper.

Finally, some researchers say our **sensitive** fingertips may have helped early humans as they searched for food. They may have helped them find the right type of food. If food was spoiled, for example, it might feel slimy. This would be a signal to not eat it.

We know a lot about how our bodies work. We can thank science for that. Still, there's a lot we don't know. Every day scientists learn more about our bodies. Maybe one day scientists will solve all the mysteries of our amazing bodies. For now, we'll keep laughing, dreaming, and yawning—even though we don't know why we do it!

| Laughter is just one of the wonderful mysteries of life that makes us human.

GLOSSARY

dominant (DOM-uh-nuhnt)—most influential or powerful

endorphin (en-DOR-fuhn)—a substance created by the brain to reduce pain

immune system (i-MYOON SISS-tuhm)—the system that protects the body from disease

motor function (MOH-tur FUHNGK-shuhn)—the movement of the body's muscles for walking, running, and other tasks

Nobel Prize (noh-BELL PRYZ)—an award given to people for outstanding work in science and other areas

oxygen (OK-suh-juhn)—a colorless gas that people and animals breathe

pandiculation (pan-dik-yuh-LEY-shuhn)—stretching and yawning at the same time

sensitive (SEN-suh-tiv)—able to feel slight changes or differences

theory (THEE-ur-ee)—an idea that explains something that is unknown

transfusion (trans-FEW-zhuhn)—the act of transferring blood into a person

universal donor (yoo-nuh-VUR-suhl DOH-nur)—someone whose blood type allows them to share their blood with anyone

whorl (WUHRL)—a fingerprint pattern in which ridges form at least one complete circle

READ MORE

Claybourne, Anna. *Why Don't Eyeballs Fall Out?: And Other Questions About the Human Body.* New York: Crabtree Publishing Company, 2021.

Clay, Kathryn. *This or That Questions About the Human Body: You Decide!* North Mankato, MN: Capstone Press, 2021.

Loh-Hagan, Virginia. *Weird Science: The Human Body.* Ann Arbor, MI: 45th Parallel Press, 2022.

INTERNET SITES

15 Facts About the Human Body!
natgeokids.com/uk/discover/science/general-science/15-facts-about-the-human-body

Human Body
kids.britannica.com/kids/article/human-body/599366

Human Body Systems for Kids!
generationgenius.com/human-body-systems-for-kids

INDEX

babies, 6, 15
blood transfusions, 23, 24
blood types, 22–25
brains, 9, 10, 17, 19, 20, 28

creativity, 19–20

diseases, 4, 9, 25
dreaming, 5, 10–13, 29

endorphins, 9

fingerprint patterns, 27
fingerprints, 26–29

health, 4, 5, 9, 11, 16, 24

immune system, 9, 24

Landsteiner, Karl, 23
laughing, 5, 6–9, 29
left-handedness, 18–21

memories, 13
motor function, 17, 18

pandiculation, 17
problem-solving, 13, 19–21

REM sleep, 10
right-handedness, 18–21

scientific method, 5
sleep, 5, 10, 11, 12, 14
sleepwalking, 12

yawning, 5, 14–17, 29

ABOUT THE AUTHOR

Myra Faye Turner is a New Orleans-based poet and author. She has written for grown-ups, but prefers writing for young readers. She has written more than two dozen fiction and nonfiction books for children and young adults, covering diverse topics like politics, the Apollo moon landing, edible insects, Black history, U.S. history, and science. When she's not writing, she spends her days reading, napping, playing Wordle, and drinking coffee.

UNSOLVED QUESTIONS ABOUT THE HUMAN BODY

Why do we yawn? Are left-handed people more creative than right-handed people? Why do we have fingerprints? When it comes to our bodies, there are a whole lot of questions we're still trying to answer. Get ready to explore the unknown and discover how scientists are working to solve the mysteries of the human body.

UNSOLVED SCIENCE

Are we alone in the universe? What's inside our planet's core? Why do we dream? The world of science is filled with unanswered questions. Dive into the unknown and discover how scientists are trying to solve the most puzzling questions about living things, the universe, our planet, and so much more.

BOOKS IN THIS SERIES

UNSOLVED QUESTIONS ABOUT EARTH

UNSOLVED QUESTIONS ABOUT THE HUMAN BODY

UNSOLVED QUESTIONS ABOUT LIVING THINGS

UNSOLVED QUESTIONS ABOUT THE UNIVERSE

U.S. $7.99 | CAN $9.99 • RL: 3–4 IL: 3–5

ISBN 978-1-66900-255-0

50799

9 781669 002550